Prayer Journal

PRAYER JOURNAL FOR WOMEN

© 2021 by Latoya Nicole. All rights reserved.

No part of this book may be used or reproduced in any manner whatsoever without the prior written permission of the author, Latoya Nicole.

ISBN: 978-1-7348797-8-0

For more information, visit us
online at www.entrepreneurscolortoo.com

This journal belongs to:

_____

A Note from the Author

Lately, the Lord has had me pray in the morning immediately after I get up before doing anything else. For a season a habit has been checking my phone when I first get up or waking up and just starting my day. He has me shifting my strategy for the purpose of keeping me open and drawing me closer to him.

I'd like to challenge you. For the next 30 days commit to making prayer something you do when you first wake up. Let's change our strategy together and honor God first.

After you pray take a moment to sit and be still. Listen to see what he's saying and write those things down as you reflect.

30 Day Prayer Challenge

Your Pastors and Leaders	Salvation for Family	Marriages	Revelation of Jesus Christ	Music Ministry
Media Ministry	A Heart to Serve	Understanding	Wisdom	Guidance
Motivation	New Opportunities	Giving thanks	A changed mind	Your Church
Your Children	The Next Generation	Self Control	Gratitude	A closer relationship with Christ
A giving spirit	Peace	Love	Joy	Meekness
Temperance	Longsuffering	Humility	The Spirit of Forgiveness	Healthy Relationships

Scriptures related to prayer:

Philippians 4:6
Be careful for nothing; but in every thing by prayer and supplication with thanksgiving let your requests be made known unto God.

Mark 11:24
Therefore I say unto you, What things soever ye desire, when ye pray, believe that ye receive them, and ye shall have them.

John 15:7
If ye abide in me, and my words abide in you, ye shall ask what ye will, and it shall be done unto you.

1 Thessalonians 5:17
Pray without ceasing.

Romans 8:26
Likewise the Spirit also helpeth our infirmities: for we know not what we should pray for as we ought: but the Spirit itself maketh intercession for us with groanings which cannot be uttered.

Maythew 6:6
But thou, when thou prayest, enter into thy closet, and when thou hast shut thy door, pray to thy Father which is in secret; and thy Father which seeth in secret shall reward thee openly.

James 5:16
Confess your faults one to another, and pray one for another, that ye may be healed. The effectual fervent prayer of a righteous man availeth much.

I will never leave nor forsake you.

Hebrews 13:5

Date: S   M   T   W   T   F   S

Lord teach me how to...

Today I am praying for...   Today I am thankful for...

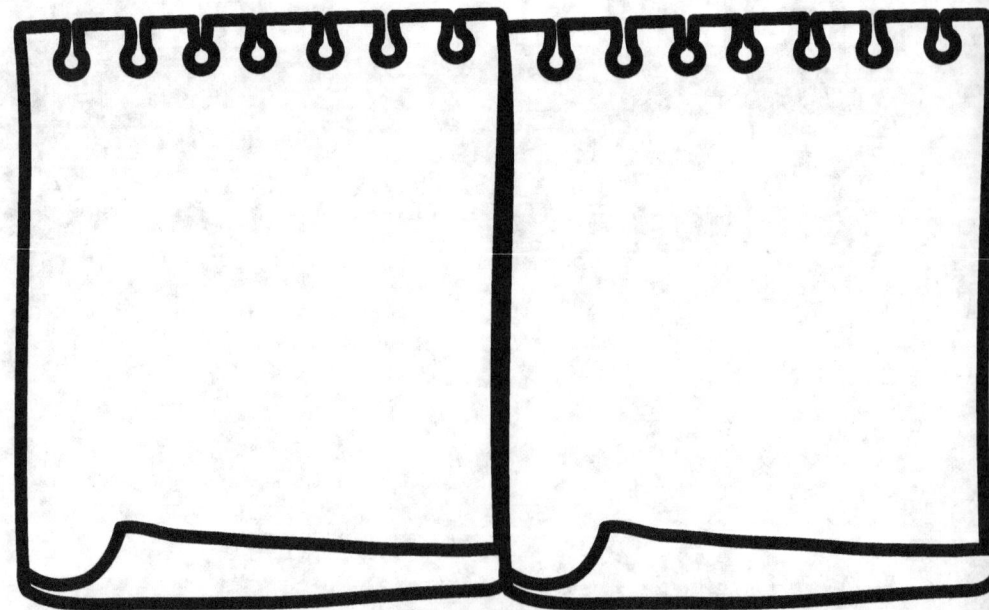

Date:　　　　　　　　　　　　　　　S   M   T   W   T   F   S

Answered prayers...

Confessions　　　　　　　　　　　　People to pray for

Date: S M T W T F S

Book of the Bible

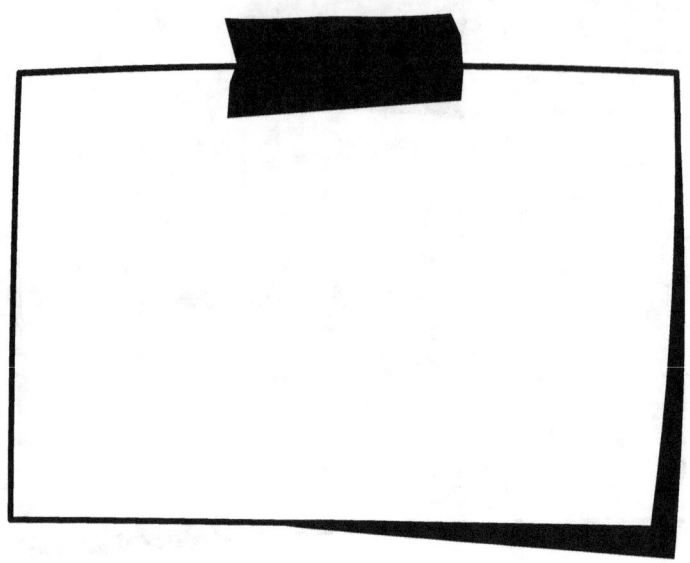

Summary of Chapter   How can I relate?

Date:

Reflection Notes

Date: S M T W T F S

Lord teach me how to...

Today I am praying for...   Today I am thankful for...

Date: S M T W T F S

Answered prayers...

Confessions People to pray for

Date: S M T W T F S

Book of the Bible

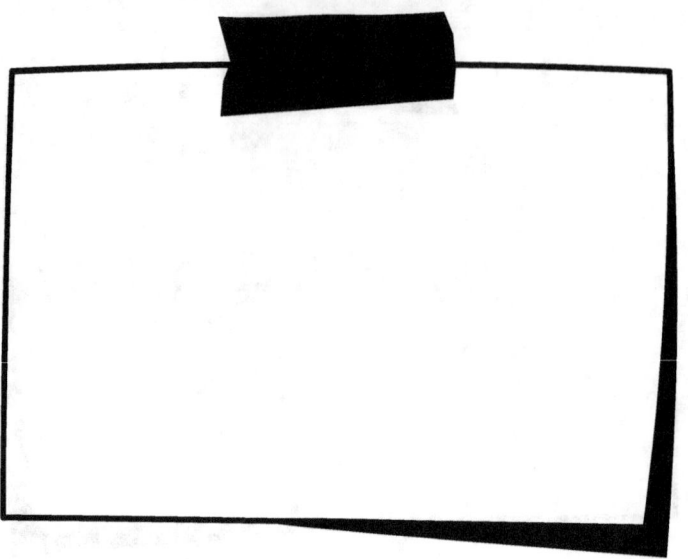

Summary of Chapter How can I relate?

Date:

Reflection Notes

Date:

S M T W T F S

Lord teach me how to...

Today I am praying for... Today I am thankful for...

Date: S M T W T F S

Answered prayers...

Confessions   People to pray for

Date: S M T W T F S

Book of the Bible

Summary of Chapter **How can I relate?**

Date:

Reflection Notes

Date: S M T W T F S

Lord teach me how to...

Today I am praying for...   Today I am thankful for...

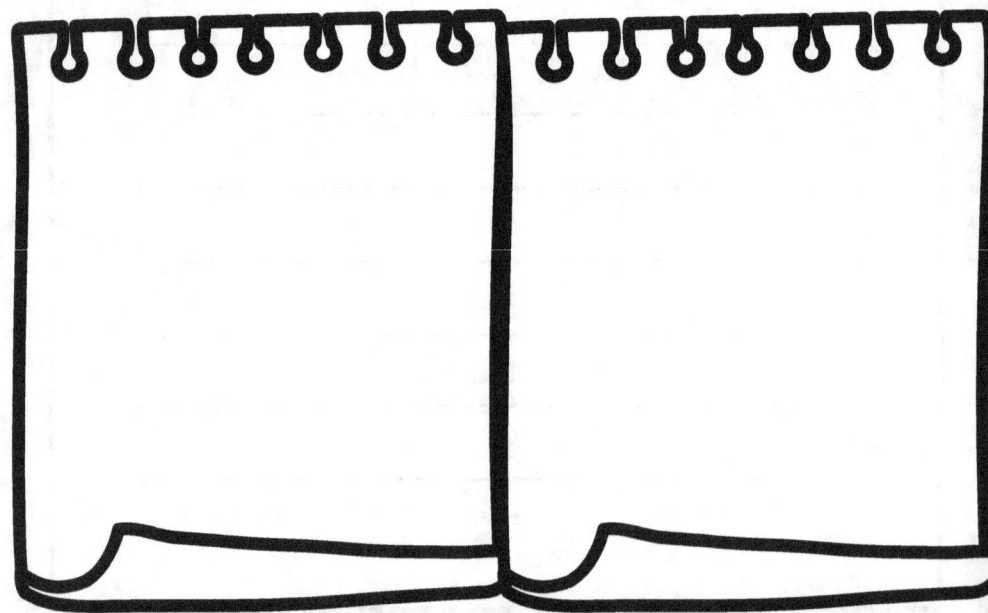

Date: S M T W T F S

Answered prayers...

Confessions   People to pray for

Date:

S M T W T F S

Book of the Bible

Summary of Chapter | How can I relate?

Date:

Reflection Notes

Date: S M T W T F S

Lord teach me how to...

Today I am praying for...   Today I am thankful for...

Date: S M T W T F S

Answered prayers...

Confessions   People to pray for

Date: S M T W T F S

Book of the Bible

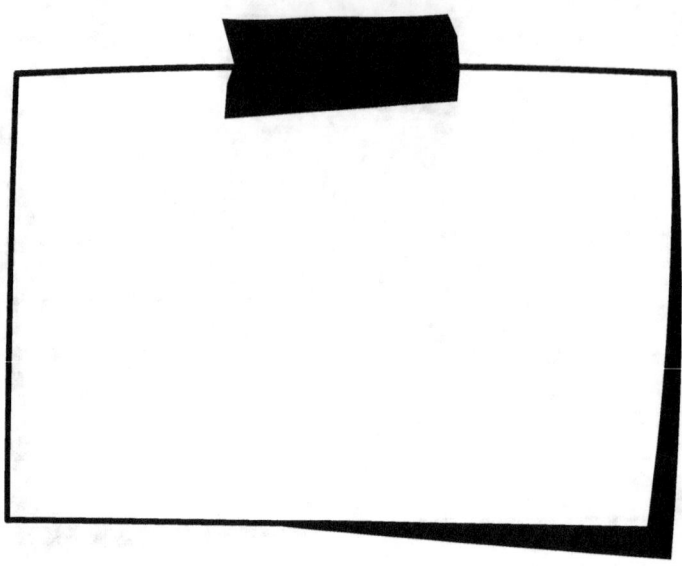

Summary of Chapter   How can I relate?

Date:

Reflection Notes

Don't be afraid. Just believe.

Mark 5:36

Date:

S M T W T F S

Lord teach me how to...

Today I am praying for...   Today I am thankful for...

Date: S M T W T F S

Answered prayers...

Confessions   People to pray for

Date: S   M   T   W   T   F   S

Book of the Bible

Summary of Chapter   **How can I relate?**

Date:

Reflection Notes

Date: S M T W T F S

Lord teach me how to...

Today I am praying for...   Today I am thankful for...

Date: S M T W T F S

Answered prayers...

Confessions   People to pray for

Date:

S M T W T F S

Book of the Bible

Summary of Chapter

How can I relate?

Date:

Reflection Notes

Date: S M T W T F S

Lord teach me how to...

Today I am praying for...   Today I am thankful for...

Date: S M T W T F S

Answered prayers...

Confessions   People to pray for

Date:

S M T W T F S

Book of the Bible

Summary of Chapter

How can I relate?

Date:

Reflection Notes

Date: S M T W T F S

Lord teach me how to...

Today I am praying for...   Today I am thankful for...

Date: S M T W T F S

Answered prayers...

Confessions   People to pray for

Date: S M T W T F S

Book of the Bible

Summary of Chapter   How can I relate?

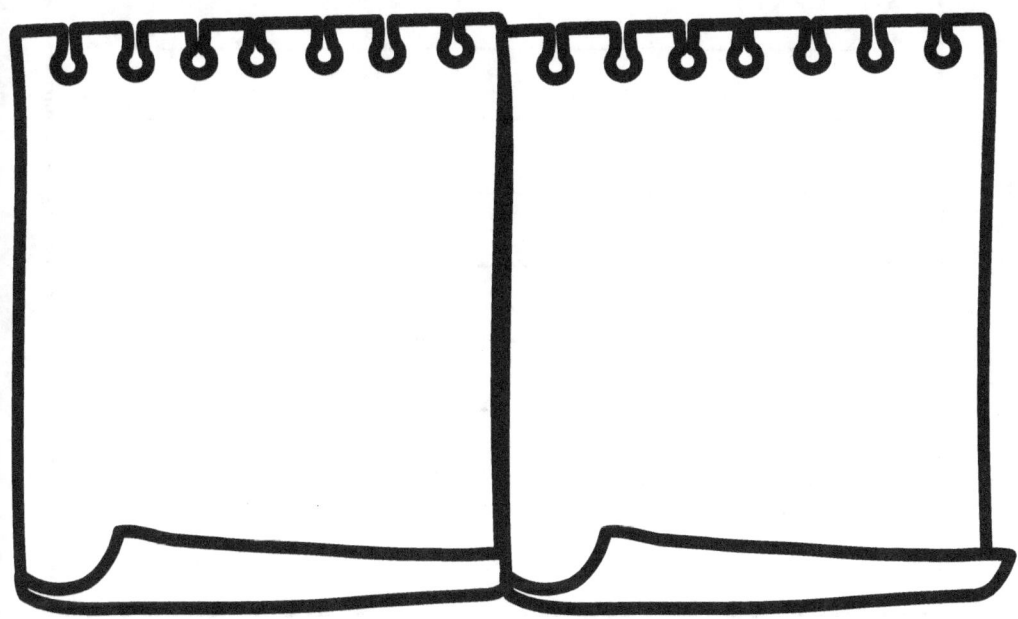

Date:

Reflection Notes

Lord you are good

Psalm 100:5

Date:

S M T W T F S

Lord teach me how to...

Today I am praying for... Today I am thankful for...

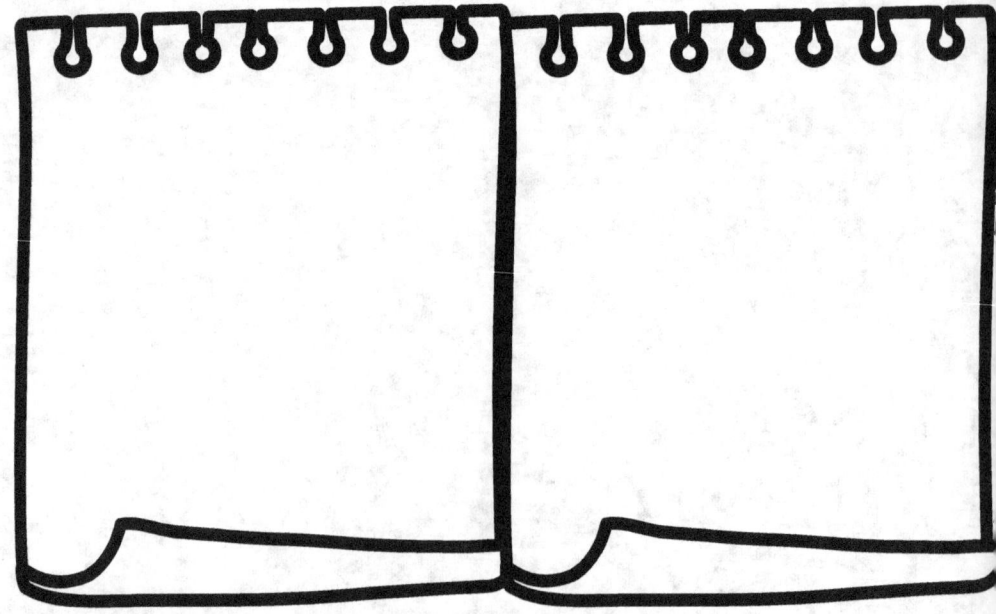

Date: S M T W T F S

Answered prayers...

Confessions   People to pray for

Date: S M T W T F S

Book of the Bible

Summary of Chapter | How can I relate?

Date:

Reflection Notes

Date: S M T W T F S

Answered prayers...

Confessions   ## People to pray for

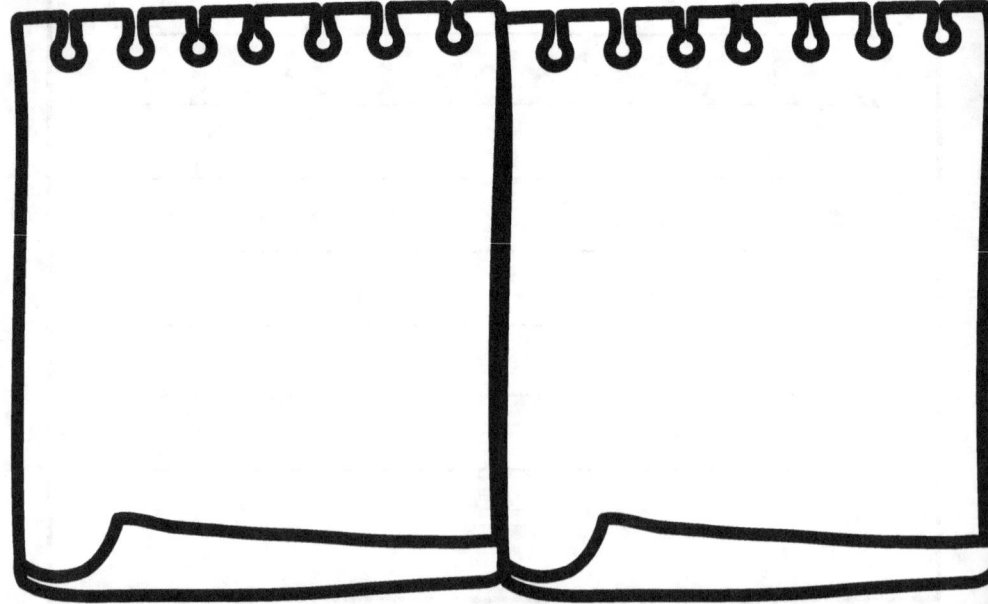

Date: S M T W T F S

Lord teach me how to...

Today I am praying for... Today I am thankful for...

Date:

S M T W T F S

Book of the Bible

Summary of Chapter

How can I relate?

Date:

Reflection Notes

Date:

S M T W T F S

Lord teach me how to...

Today I am praying for...   Today I am thankful for...

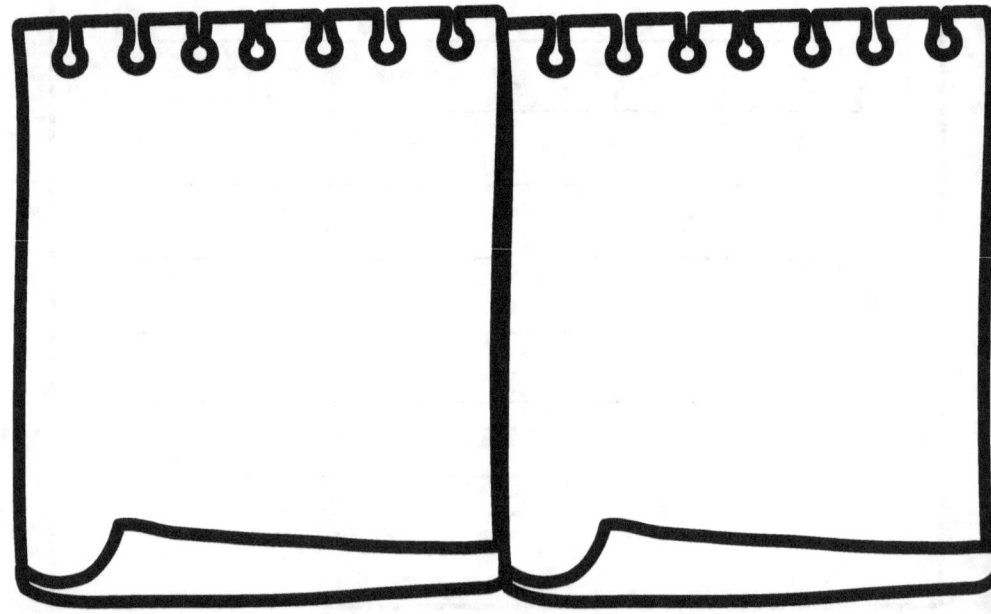

Date:

S M T W T F S

Answered prayers...

Confessions

People to pray for

Date: S M T W T F S

Book of the Bible

Summary of Chapter   How can I relate?

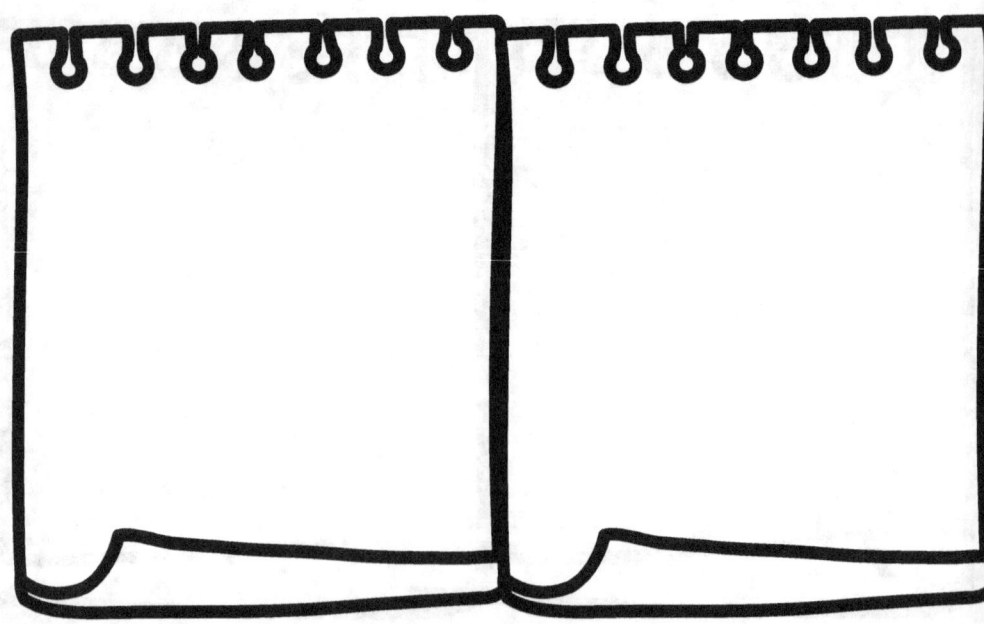

Date:

Reflection Notes

Date: S M T W T F S

Lord teach me how to...

Today I am praying for...   Today I am thankful for...

Date:

S M T W T F S

Answered prayers...

Confessions

People to pray for

Date: S M T W T F S

Book of the Bible

Summary of Chapter How can I relate?

Date:

Reflection Notes

Ask, and it shall be given you; seek, and ye. shall find; knock, and it shall be opened unto you.

Matthew 7:7

Date:

S M T W T F S

Lord teach me how to...

Today I am praying for...   Today I am thankful for...

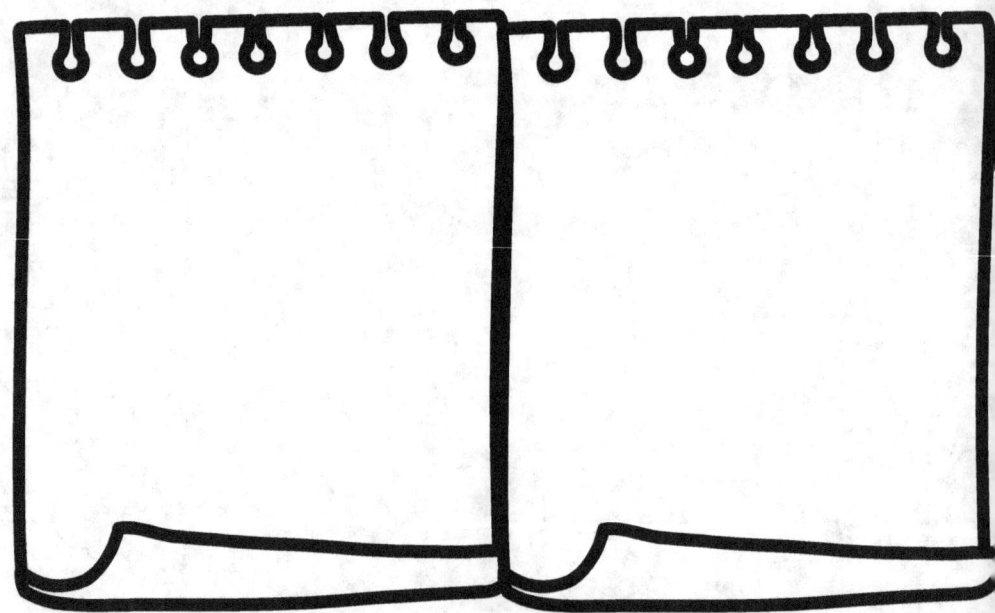

Date: S M T W T F S

Answered prayers...

Confessions   People to pray for

Date: S M T W T F S

Book of the Bible

Summary of Chapter | How can I relate?

Date:

Reflection Notes

Date:

S M T W T F S

Lord teach me how to...

Today I am praying for...   Today I am thankful for...

Date: S M T W T F S

Answered prayers...

Confessions People to pray for

Date: S M T W T F S

Book of the Bible

Summary of Chapter   How can I relate?

Date:

Reflection Notes

Date: S M T W T F S

Lord teach me how to...

Today I am praying for... Today I am thankful for...

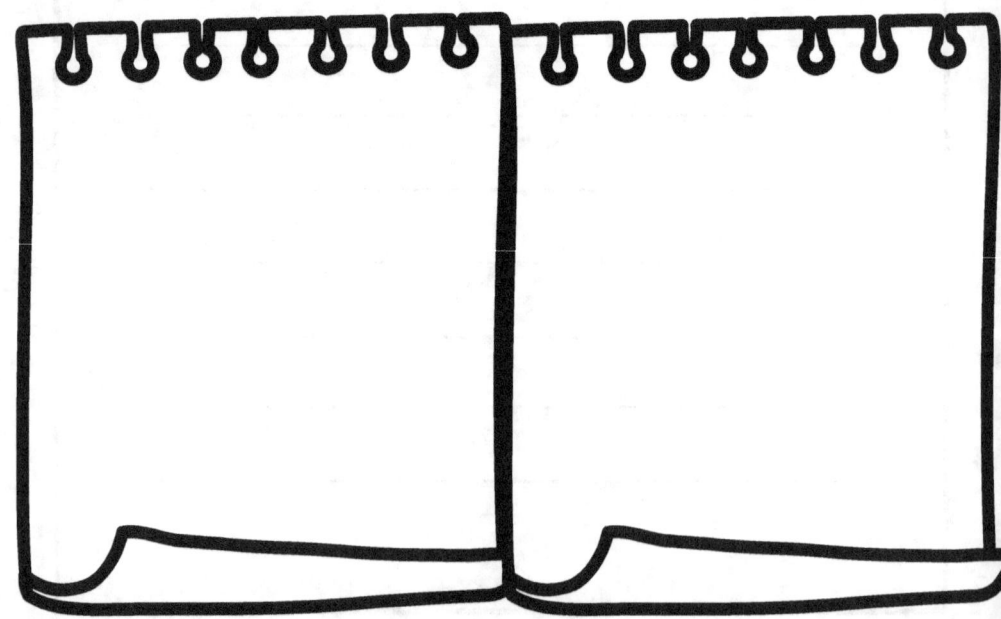

Date: S M T W T F S

Answered prayers...

Confessions   People to pray for

Date: S M T W T F S

Book of the Bible

Summary of Chapter   How can I relate?

Date:

Reflection Notes

Date:　　　　　　　　　　　　　　　　S M T W T F S

Lord teach me how to...

Today I am praying for...　　　　　Today I am thankful for...

Date: S M T W T F S

Answered prayers...

Confessions   People to pray for

Date: S M T W T F S

Book of the Bible

Summary of Chapter   How can I relate?

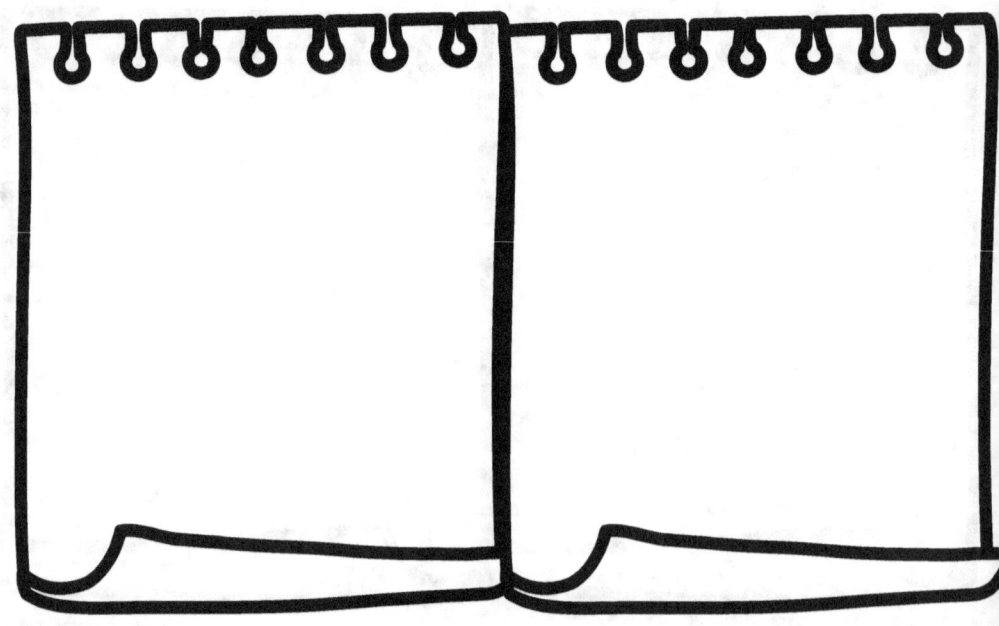

Date:

Reflection Notes

Date: S M T W T F S

Lord teach me how to...

Today I am praying for...   Today I am thankful for...

Date:　　　　　　　　　　　　　S M T W T F S

Answered prayers...

Confessions　　　　　　　　　People to pray for

Date:　　　　　　　　　　　　　　　　　S M T W T F S

Book of the Bible

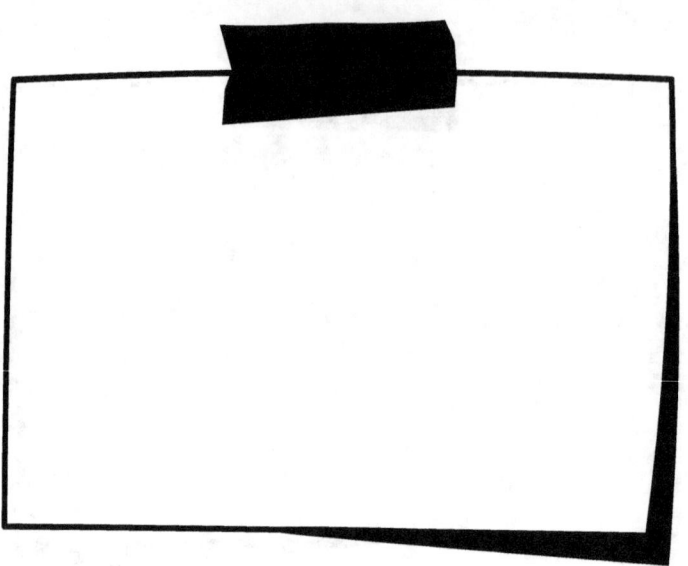

Summary of Chapter　　　　　　　How can I relate?

Date:

Reflection Notes

Love beareth all things, believeth all things, hopeth all things, endureth all things.

1 Corinthians 13:7

Date: S   M   T   W   T   F   S

Lord teach me how to...

Today I am praying for...   Today I am thankful for...

Date: S M T W T F S

Answered prayers...

Confessions People to pray for

Date:

S M T W T F S

Book of the Bible

Summary of Chapter

How can I relate?

Date:

Reflection Notes

Date:

S M T W T F S

Lord teach me how to...

Today I am praying for... Today I am thankful for...

Date: S   M   T   W   T   F   S

Answered prayers...

Confessions   People to pray for

Date:

S M T W T F S

Book of the Bible

Summary of Chapter

How can I relate?

Date:

Reflection Notes

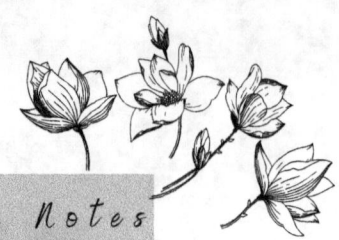

Date:

S M T W T F S

Lord teach me how to...

Today I am praying for...   Today I am thankful for...

Date: S M T W T F S

Answered prayers...

Confessions People to pray for

Date:

S M T W T F S

Book of the Bible

Summary of Chapter

How can I relate?

Date:

Reflection Notes

Date: S   M   T   W   T   F   S

Lord teach me how to...

Today I am praying for...   *Today I am thankful for...*

Date:

S M T W T F S

Answered prayers...

Confessions

People to pray for

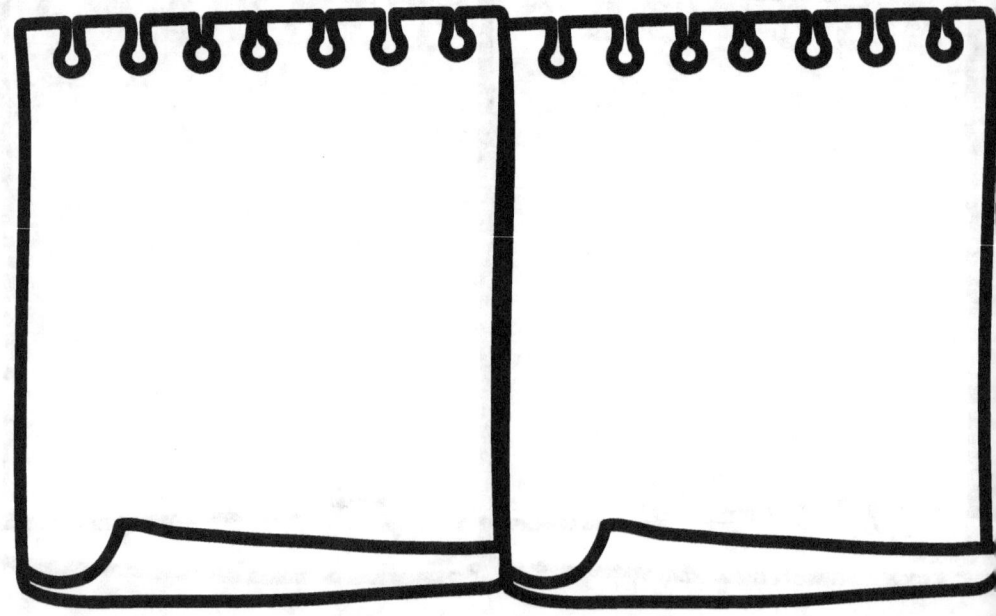

Date: S M T W T F S

Book of the Bible

Summary of Chapter   **How can I relate?**

Date:

Reflection Notes

Be Still and Know that I am God

Psalm 46:10

Date:

S M T W T F S

Lord teach me how to...

Today I am praying for...   Today I am thankful for...

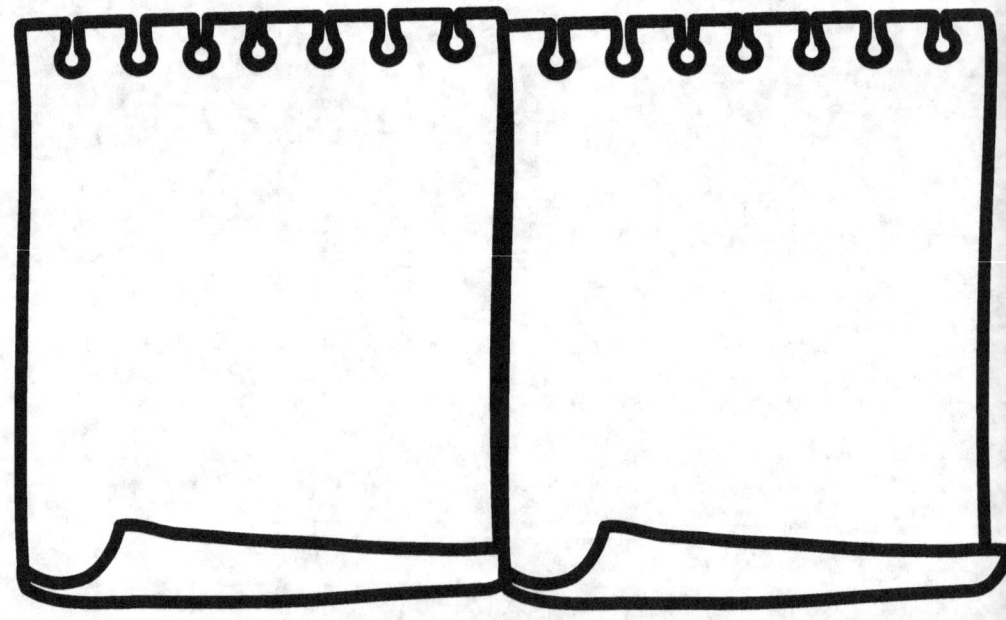

Date:　　　　　　　　　　　　　　　S M T W T F S

Answered prayers...

Confessions　　　　　　　　　People to pray for

Date: S M T W T F S

Book of the Bible

Summary of Chapter   **How can I relate?**

Date:

Reflection Notes

Date: S M T W T F S

Answered prayers...

Confessions   People to pray for

Date: S M T W T F S

Lord teach me how to...

Today I am praying for... Today I am thankful for...

Date: S M T W T F S

Book of the Bible

Summary of Chapter   How can I relate?

Date:

Reflection Notes

Date:

S M T W T F S

Lord teach me how to...

Today I am praying for...   Today I am thankful for...

Date: S M T W T F S

Answered prayers...

Confessions   People to pray for

Date:

S M T W T F S

Book of the Bible

Summary of Chapter

How can I relate?

Date:

Reflection Notes

Date: S M T W T F S

Lord teach me how to...

Today I am praying for...   Today I am thankful for...

Date: S M T W T F S

Answered prayers...

Confessions   People to pray for

Date:

S M T W T F S

Book of the Bible

Summary of Chapter

How can I relate?

Date:

Reflection Notes

www.ingramcontent.com/pod-product-compliance
Lightning Source LLC
Chambersburg PA
CBHW052207090526
44583CB00016BA/1772